I0075175

THE LIMITATIONS OF
MARGINAL UTILITY

BY

THORSTEIN VEBLEN

Copyright © 2013 Read Books Ltd.
This book is copyright and may not be
reproduced or copied in any way without
the express permission of the publisher in writing

British Library Cataloguing-in-Publication Data
A catalogue record for this book is available from the
British Library

Contents

Thorstein Veblen

Thorstein Bunde Veblen was born Torsten Bunde Veblen on 30th July 1857 in Cato, Wisconsin, United States, to Norwegian immigrant parents.

Veblen grew up on his parents farm in Nerstrand, Minnesota. This area and others like it were known as little Norways due to the religious and cultural traditions that had been imported from the old country. Although Norwegian was his first language, the young Veblen learned English from neighbours and at school.

His parents put a lot of emphasis on education and hard work and at age seventeen he was sent to study at Carleton College Academy. It was there that he met John Bates Clark (1847–1938) who went on to become a leader in the new field of neoclassical economics. Upon graduating Veblen conducted graduate work under Charles Sanders Pierce (the founder of the pragmatist school in philosophy) at John Hopkins University. He then moved to Yale in 1884 to take a Ph.D. and completed his dissertation on "Ethical Grounds of a Doctrine of Retribution."

Upon leaving Yale he was unable to find a employment. This was partly due to prejudice against Norwegians, and partly because most universities considered him insufficiently educated in Christianity; most academics at the time held divinity degrees. Due to this, Veblen returned to the family farm – ostensibly to recover from malaria – and spent six years there reading voraciously. However, in 1891 he was accepted to study economics as a graduate student at Cornell University. From here on his academic career took off, obtaining his first professional appointment at the University of Chicago – where in 1900 he was promoted to assistant professor – and from there moving on work at institutions including Stanford University and the University of Missouri.

Veblen drew from the work of 19th century intellectuals such as Charles Darwin and Herbert Spencer to develop a 20th century theory of evolutionary economics. He described economic behaviour as socially determined and saw economic organization as a process of ongoing evolution. In his work *The Theory of the Leisure Class* (1899) he outlined how rich and poor alike, attempt to impress others and seek to gain advantage through what Veblen coined "conspicuous consumption" and the ability to engage in "conspicuous leisure." In *The Theory of Business Enterprise* (1904) he used evolutionary analysis to explain the growth of business combinations and trusts.

In the 21st century his ideas have come back into the spotlight as a valid approach for studying the intricacies of economic systems and his theory that humans do not rationally pursue value and utility is one of the cornerstones of the modern discipline of behavioural economics. Veblen made a lasting contribution to his field and has influenced many scholars that have followed him.

Thorstein Veblen died in California on 3rd August 1929, less than three months before the crash of the U.S. Stock market crash which led to the great depression.

THE LIMITATIONS
OF MARGINAL UTILITY

THORSTEIN VEBLEN
1909

JOURNAL OF POLITICAL ECONOMY,
VOLUME 17.

The limitations of the marginal-utility economics are sharp and characteristic. It is from first to last a doctrine of value, and in point of form and method it is a theory of valuation. The whole system, therefore, lies within the theoretical field of distribution, and it has but a secondary bearing on any other economic phenomena than those of distribution -- the term being taken in its accepted sense of pecuniary distribution, or distribution in point of ownership. Now and again an attempt is made to extend the use of the principle of marginal utility beyond this range, so as to apply it to questions of production, but hitherto without sensible effect, and necessarily so. The most ingenious and the most promising of such attempts have been those of Mr Clark, whose work marks the extreme range of endeavor and the extreme degree of success in so seeking to turn a postulate of distribution to account for a theory of production. But the outcome has been a doctrine of the production of values, and value, in Mr Clark's as in other utility systems, is a matter of valuation; which throws the whole excursion back into the field of distribution. Similarly, as regards attempts to make use of this principle in an analysis of the phenomena of consumption, the best results arrived at are some formulation of the pecuniary distribution of consumption goods.

Within this limited range marginal utility theory is of a wholly statical character. It offers no theory of a movement of any kind, being occupied with the adjustment of values to a given situation. Of this, again, no more convincing illustration need be had than is afforded by the work of Mr. Clark, which is not excelled in point of earnestness, perseverance, or insight. For all their use of the term "dynamic", neither Mr. Clark nor any of his associates in this line of research have yet contributed anything at all appreciable to a theory of genesis, growth, sequence, change, process, or the like, in economic life. They have had something to say as to the bearing which given economic changes, accepted as premises, may have on economic valuation, and so on distribution; but as to the causes of change or the unfolding sequence of the phenomena of economic life they have had nothing to say hitherto; nor can they, since their theory is not drawn in causal terms but in terms of teleology.

In all this the marginal utility school is substantially at one with the classical economics of the nineteenth century, the difference between the two being that the former is confined within narrower limits and sticks more consistently to its teleological premises. Both are teleological, and neither can consistently admit arguments from cause to effect in the formulation of their main articles of theory. Neither can deal theoretically with phenomena of change, but at the most only with rational adjustment to change which may be supposed to have supervened.

To the modern scientist the phenomena of growth and change are the most obtrusive and most consequential facts observable in economic life. For an understanding of modern economic life the technological advance of the past two centuries -- e.g., the growth of the industrial arts -- is of the first importance; but marginal utility theory does not bear on this matter, nor does this matter bear on marginal utility theory. As a means of theoretically accounting for this technological movement in the past or in the present, or even as a means of formally, technically stating it as an element in the current economic situation, that doctrine and all its works are altogether idle. The like is true for the sequence of change that is going forward in the pecuniary relations of modern life; the hedonistic postulate and its propositions of differential utility neither have served nor can serve an inquiry into these phenomena of growth, although the whole body of marginal utility economics lies within the range of these pecuniary phenomena. It has nothing to say to the growth of business usages and expedients or to the concomitant changes in the principles of conduct which govern the pecuniary relations of men, which condition and are conditioned by these altered relations of business life or which bring them to pass.

It is characteristic of the school that whatever an element of the cultural fabric, an institution or any institutional phenomenon, is involved in the facts with which the theory is occupied, such institutional facts are taken for granted, denied, or explained away. If it is a question of price, there is offered an explanation of how exchanges may take place with such effect as to leave money and price out of the account. If it is a question of credit, the effect of credit extension on business traffic is left on one side and there is an explanation of how the borrower and lender cooperate to smooth out their respective income streams of consumable goods or sensations of consumption. The failure of the school in this respect is consistent and comprehensive. And yet these economists are lacking neither in intelligence nor in information. They are, indeed, to be credited, commonly, with a wide range of information and an exact control of materials, as well as with a very alert interest in what is going on; and apart from their theoretical pronouncements the members of the school habitually profess the sanest and most intelligent views of current practical questions, even when these questions touch matters of institutional growth and decay.

The infirmity of this theoretical scheme lies in its postulates which confine the inquiry to generalisations of the teleological or "deductive" order. These postulates, together with the point of view and logical method that follow from them, the marginal utility school shares with other economists of the classical line -- for this school is but a branch or derivative of the English classical economists of the nineteenth century. The substantial difference between this school and the generality of classical economists lies mainly in the fact that in the marginal utility economics the common postulates are more consistently adhered to at the same time that they are more neatly defined and their limitations are more adequately realized. Both the classical school is general and its specialized variant, the marginal utility school, in particular, take as their common point of departure the traditional psychology of the early nineteenth century hedonists, which is accepted as a matter of course or of common notoriety and is held quite uncritically. The central and well defined tenet so held is that of the hedonistic calculus. Under the guidance of this tenet and of the other psychological conceptions associated and consonant with it, human conduct is conceived of and interpreted as a rational response to the exigencies of the situation in which mankind is placed; as regards economic conduct it is such a rational and unprejudiced response to the stimulus of anticipated pleasure and pain -- being, typically and in the main, a response to the promptings of anticipated pleasure, for the hedonists of the nineteenth century and of the marginal utility school are in the main of an optimistic temper.1 Mankind is, on the whole and normally, (conceived to be) clearsighted and farsighted in its appreciation of future sensuous gains and losses, although there may be some (inconsiderable) difference between men in this respect. Men's activities differ, therefore, (inconsiderably) in respect of the alertness of the response and the nicety of adjustment of irksome pain cost to apprehended future sensuous gain; but, on the whole, no other ground or line or guidance of conduct than this rationalistic calculus falls properly within the cognizance of the economic hedonists. Such a theory can take account of conduct only in so far as it is rational conduct, guided by deliberate and exhaustively intelligent choice -- wise adaption to the demands of the main chance.

The external circumstances which condition conduct are variable, of course, and so they will have a varying effect upon conduct; but their variation is, in effect, construed to be of such a character only as to vary the degree of strain to which the human agent is subject by contact with these external circumstances. The cultural elements involved in the theoretical scheme, elements that are of the nature of institutions, human relations governed by use and wont in whatever kind and connection, are not subject to inquiry but are taken from granted as preexisting in a finished, typical form and as making up a normal and definite economic situation, under which and in terms of which human intercourse is necessarily carried on. This cultural situation comprises a few large and simple articles of institutional furniture, together with their logical implications or corollaries; but it includes nothing of the consequences or effects caused by these institutional elements. The cultural elements so tacitly postulated as immutable conditions precedent to economic life are ownership and free contract, together with such other features of the scheme of natural rights as are implied in the exercise of these. These cultural products are, for the purpose of the theory, conceived to be given a priori in unmitigated force. They are part of the nature of things; so that there is no need of accounting for them or inquiring into them, as to how they have come to be such as they are, or how and why they have changed and are changing, or what effect all this may have on the relations of men who live by or under this cultural situation.

Evidently the acceptance of these immutable premises, tacitly, because uncritically and as a matter of course, by hedonistic economics gives the science a distinctive character and places it in contrast with other sciences whose premises are of a different order. As has already been indicated, the premises in question, so far as they are peculiar to the hedonistic economics, are (a) a certain institutional situation, the substantial feature of which is the natural right of ownership, and (b) the hedonistic calculus. The distinctive character given to this system of theory by these postulates and by the point of view resulting from their acceptance may be summed up broadly and concisely in saying that the theory is confined to the ground of sufficient reason instead of proceeding on the ground of efficient cause. The contrary is true of modern science, generally (except mathematics), particularly of such sciences as have to do with the phenomena of life and growth. The difference may seem trivial. It is serious only in its consequences. The two methods of inference -- from sufficient reason and from efficient cause -- are out of touch with one another and there is no transition from one to the other; no method of converting the procedure or the results of the one into those of the other. The immediate consequence is that the resulting economic theory is of a teleological character -- "deductive" or "a priori" as it is often called -- instead of being drawn in terms of cause and effect. The relation sought by this theory among the facts with which it is occupied is the control exercised by future (apprehended) events over present conduct. Current phenomena are dealt with as conditioned by their future consequences; and in strict marginal-utility theory they can be dealt with only in respect of their control of the present by consideration of the future. Such a (logical)

12

relation of control or guidance between the future and the present of course involves an exercise of intelligence, a taking thought, and hence an intelligent agent through whose discriminating forethought the apprehended future may affect the current course of events; unless, indeed, one were to admit something in the way of a providential elements, the relation of sufficient reason runs by way of the interested discrimination, the forethought, of an agent who takes thought of the future and guides his present activity by regard for this future. The relation of sufficient reason runs only from the (apprehended) future into the present, and it is solely of an intellectual, subjective, personal, teleological character and force; while the relation of cause and effect runs only in the contrary direction, and it is solely of an objective, impersonal materialistic character and force. The modern scheme of knowledge, on the whole, rests for its definitive ground, on the relation of cause and effect; the relation of sufficient reason being admitted only provisionally and as a proximate factor in the analysis, always with the unambiguous reservation that the analysis must ultimately come to rest in terms of cause and effect. The merits of this scientific animus, of course, do not concern the present argument.

Now, it happens that the relation of sufficient reason enters very substantially into human conduct. It is this element of discriminating forethought that distinguishes human conduct from brute behavior. And since the economist's subject of inquiry is this human conduct, that relation necessarily comes in for a large share of his attention in any theoretical formulation of economic phenomena, whether hedonistic or otherwise. But while modern science at large has made the causal relation the sole ultimate ground of theoretical formulation; and while the other sciences that deal with human life admit the relation of sufficient reason as a proximate, supplementary, or intermediate ground, subsidiary, and subservient to the argument from cause and effect; economics has had the misfortune -- as seen from the scientific point of view -- to let the former supplant the latter. It is, of course, true that human conduct is distinguished from other natural phenomena by the human faculty for taking thought, and any science that has to do with human conduct must face the patent fact that the details of such conduct consequently fall into the teleological form; but it is the peculiarity of the hedonistic economics that by force of its postulated its attention is confined to this teleological bearing of conduct alone. It deals with this conduct only in so far as it may be construed in rationalistic, teleological terms of calculation and choice. But it is at the same time no less true that human conduct, economic or otherwise, is subject to the sequence of cause and effect, by force of such elements as habituation and conventional requirements. But facts of this order, which are to modern science of graver interest than the teleological details of conduct, necessarily fall outside the attention of the hedonistic economist, because they cannot be construed in terms of sufficient reason, such as his postulates demand, or be fitted into a scheme of teleological doctrines.

There is, therefore, no call to impugn these premises of the marginal-utility economics within their field. They commend themselves to all serious and uncritical persons at first glance. They are principles of action which underlie the current, business-like scheme of economic life, and as such, as practical grounds of conduct, they are not to be called in question without questioning the existing law and order. As a matter of course, men order their lives by these principles and, practically, entertain no question of their stability and finality. That is what is meant by calling them institutions; they are settled habits of thought common to the generality of men. But it would be mere absentmindedness in any student of civilization therefore to admit that these or any other human institutions have this stability which is currently imputed to them or that they are in this way intrinsic to the nature of things. The acceptance by the economists of these or other institutional elements as given and immutable limits their inquiry in a particular and decisive way. It shuts off the inquiry at the point where the modern scientific interest sets in. The institutions in question are no doubt good for their purpose as institutions, but they are not good as premises for a scientific inquiry into the nature, origin, growth, and effects of these institutions and of the mutations which they undergo and which they bring to pass in the community's scheme of life.

To any modern scientist interested in economic phenomena, the chain of cause and effect in which any given phase of human culture is involved, as well as the cumulative changes wrought in the fabric of human conduct itself by the habitual activity of mankind, are matters of more engrossing and more abiding interest than the method of inference by which an individual is presumed invariably to balance pleasure and pain under given conditions that are presumed to be normal and invariable. The former are questions of the life-history of the race or the community, questions of cultural growth and of the fortunes of generations; while the latter is a question of individual casuistry in the face of a given situation that may arise in the course of this cultural growth. The former bear on the continuity and mutations of that scheme of conduct whereby mankind deals with its material means of life; the latter, if it is conceived in hedonistic terms, concerns a disconnected episode in the sensuous experience of an individual member of such a community.

In so far as modern science inquires into the phenomena of life, whether inanimate, brute, or human, it is occupied about questions of genesis and cumulative change, and it converges upon a theoretical formulation in the shape of a life-history drawn in causal terms. In so far as it is a science in the current sense of the term, any science, such as economics, which has to do with human conduct, becomes a genetic inquiry into the human scheme of life; and where, as in economics, the subject of inquiry is the conduct of man in his dealings with the material means of life, the science is necessarily an inquiry into the life-history of material civilization, on a more or less extended or restricted plan. Not that the economist's inquiry isolates material civilization from all other phases and bearings of human culture, and so studies the motions of an abstractly conceived "economic man." On the contrary, no theoretical inquiry into this material civilization in its causal, that is to say, its genetic, relations to other phases and bearings of the cultural complex; without studying it as it is wrought upon by other lines of cultural growth and as working its effects in these other lines. But in so far as the inquiry is economic science, specifically, the attention will converge upon the scheme of material life and will take in other phases of civilization only in their correlation with the scheme of material civilization.

Like all human culture this material civilization is a scheme of institutions -- institutional fabric and institutional growth. But institutions are an outgrowth of habit. The growth of culture is a cumulative sequence of habituation, and the ways and means of it are the habitual response of human nature to exigencies that vary incontinently, cumulatively, but with something of a consistent sequence in the cumulative variations that so go forward, -- incontinently, because each new move creates a new situation which induces a further new variation in the habitual manner of response; cumulatively, because each new situation is a variation of what has gone before it and embodies as causal factors all that has been effected by what went before; consistently, because the underlying traits of human nature (propensities, aptitudes, and what not) by force of which the response takes place, and on the ground of which the habituation takes effect, remain substantially unchanged.

Evidently an economic inquiry which occupies itself exclusively with the movements of this consistent, elemental human nature under given, stable institutional conditions -- such as is the case with the current hedonistic economics -- can reach statical results alone; since it makes abstraction from those elements that make for anything but a statical result. On the other hand an adequate theory of economic conduct, even for statical purposes, cannot be drawn in terms of the individual simply -- as is the case in the marginal-utility economics -- because it cannot be drawn in terms of the underlying traits of human nature simply; since the response that goes to make up human conduct takes place under institutional norms and only under stimuli that have an institutional bearing; for the situation that provokes and inhibits action in any given case is itself in great part of institutional, cultural derivation. Then, too, the phenomena of human life occur only as phenomena of the life of a group or community; only under stimuli due to contact with the group and only under the (habitual) control exercised by canons of conduct imposed by the group's scheme of life. Not only is the individual's conduct hedged about and directed by his habitual relations to his fellows in the group, but these relations, being of an institutional character, vary as the institutional scheme varies. The wants and desires, the end and aim, the ways and means, the amplitude and drift of the individual's conduct are functions of an institutional variable that is of a highly complex and wholly unstable character.

The growth and mutations of the institutional fabric are an outcome of the conduct of the individual members of the group, since it is out of the experience of the individuals, through the habituation of individuals, that institutions arise; and it is in this same experience that these institutions act to direct and define the aims and end of conduct. It is, of course, on individuals that the system of institutions imposes those conventional standards, ideals, and canons of conduct that make up the community's scheme of life. Scientific inquiry in this field, therefore, must deal with individual conduct and must formulate its theoretical results in terms of individual conduct. But such an inquiry can serve the purposes of a genetic theory only if and in so far as this individual conduct is attended to in those respects in which it counts toward habituation, and so toward change (or stability) of the institutional fabric, on the one hand, and in those respects in which it is prompted and guided by the received institutional conceptions and ideals on the other hand. The postulates of marginal utility, and the hedonistic preconceptions generally, fail at this point in that they confine the attention to such bearings of economic conduct as are conceived not to be conditioned by habitual standards and ideals and to have no effect in the way of habituation. They disregard or abstract from the causal sequence of propensity and habituation in economic life and exclude from theoretical inquiry all such interest in the facts of cultural growth, in order to attend to those features of the case that are conceived to be idle in this respect. All such facts of institutional force and growth are put on one side as not being germane to pure theory; they are to be taken account of, if at all, by afterthought, by a more or less vague and general allowance for inconsequential disturbances due to occasional human infirmity. Certain institutional phenomena, it is true, are comprised among the premises of the hedonists, as has been noted above; but they are included as postulates a priori. So the institution of ownership is taken into the inquiry not as a factor of growth or an element subject to change, but as one of the primordial and immutable facts of the order of nature, underlying the hedonistic calculus. Property, ownership, is presumed as the basis of hedonistic discrimination and it is conceived to be given in its finished (nineteenth-century) scope and force. There is not thought either of a conceivable growth of this definitive nineteenth-century institution out of a cruder past or of any conceivable cumulative change in the scope and force of ownership in the present or future. Nor is it conceived that the presence of this institutional element in men's economic relations in any degree affects or disguises the hedonistic calculus, or that its pecuniary conceptions and standards in any degree standardize, color, mitigate, or divert the hedonistic calculator from the direct and unhampered quest of the net sensuous gain. While the institution of property is included in this way among the postulates of the theory, and is even presumed to be ever-present in the economic situation, it is allowed to have no force in shaping economic conduct, which is conceived to run its course to its hedonistic outcome as if no such institutional factor intervened between the impulse and its realization. The institution of property, together with all the range of pecuniary conceptions that belong under it and that cluster about it, are presumed to give rise to no habitual or conventional canons of conduct or standards of valuation, no proximate ends, ideals, or aspirations. All pecuniary notions arising from ownership are treated simply as expedients of computation which mediate between the pain-cost and the pleasure-gain of hedonistic choice, without lag, leak, or friction; they are conceived simply as the immutably correct, God-given notation of the hedonistic calculus.

The modern economic situation is a business situation, in that economic activity of all kinds is commonly controlled by business considerations. The exigencies of modern life are commonly pecuniary exigencies. That is to say they are exigencies of the ownership of property. Productive efficiency and distributive gain are both rated in terms of price. Business considerations are considerations of price, and pecuniary exigencies of whatever kind in the modern communities are exigencies of price. The current economic situation is a price system. Economic institutions in the modern civilized scheme of life are (prevailing) institutions of the price system. The accountancy to which all phenomena of modern economic life are amenable is an accountancy in terms of price; and by the current convention there is no other recognized scheme of accountancy, no other rating, either in law or in fact, to which the facts of modern life are held amenable. Indeed, so great and pervading a force has this habit (institution) of pecuniary accountancy become that it extends, often as a matter of course, to many facts which properly have no pecuniary bearing and no pecuniary magnitude, as, e.g., works of art, science, scholarship, and religion. More or less freely and fully, the price system dominates the current common sense in its appreciation and rating of these non-pecuniary ramifications of modern culture; and this in spite of the fact that, on reflection, all men of normal intelligence will freely admit that these matters lie outside the scope of pecuniary valuation.

Current popular taste and the popular sense of merit and demerit are notoriously affected in some degree by pecuniary considerations. It is a matter of common notoriety, not to be denied or explained away, that pecuniary ("commercial") tests and standards are habitually made use of outside of commercial interests proper. Precious stones, it is admitted, even by hedonistic economists, are more esteemed than they would be if they were more plentiful and cheaper. A wealthy person meets with more consideration and enjoys a larger measure of good repute than would fall to the share of the same person with the same habit of mind and body and the same record of good and evil deeds if he were poorer. It may well be that this current "commercialization" of taste and appreciation has been overstated by superficial and hasty critics of contemporary life, but it will not be denied that there is a modicum of truth in the allegation. Whatever substance it has, much or little, is due to carrying over into other fields of interest the habitual conceptions induced by dealing with and thinking of pecuniary matters. These "commercial" conceptions of merit and demerit are derived from business experience. The pecuniary tests and standards so applied outside of business transactions and relations are not reducible to sensuous terms of pleasure and pain. Indeed, it may, e.g., be true, as is commonly believed, that the contemplation of a wealthy neighbor's pecuniary superiority yields painful rather than pleasurable sensations as an immediate result; but it is equally true that such a wealthy neighbor is, on the whole, more highly regarded and more considerately treated than another neighbor who differs from the former only in being less enviable in respect of wealth.

It is the institution of property that gives rise to these habitual grounds of discrimination, and in modern times, when wealth is counted in terms of money, it is in terms of money value that these tests and standards of pecuniary excellence are applied. This much will be admitted. Pecuniary institutions induce pecuniary habits of thought which affect men's discrimination outside of pecuniary matters; but the hedonistic interpretation alleges that such pecuniary habits of thought do not affect men's discrimination in pecuniary matters. Although the institutional scheme of the price system visibly dominates the modern community's thinking in matters that lie outside the economic interest, the hedonistic economists insist, in effect, that this institutional scheme must be accounted of no effect within that range of activity to which it owes its genesis, growth, and persistence. The phenomena of business, which are peculiarly and uniformly phenomena of price, are in the scheme of the hedonistic theory reduced to non-pecuniary hedonistic terms and the theoretical formulation is carried out as if pecuniary conceptions had no force within the traffic in which such conceptions originate. It is admitted that preoccupation with commercial interests has "commercialised" the rest of modern life, but the "commercialization" of commerce is not admitted. Business transactions and computations in pecuniary terms, such as loans, discounts, and capitalisation, are without hesitation or abatement converted into terms of hedonistic utility, and conversely.

It may be needless to take exception to such conversion from pecuniary into sensuous terms, for the theoretical purpose for which it is habitually make; although, if need were, it might not be excessively difficult to show that the whole hedonistic basis of such a conversion is a psychological misconception. But it is to the remoter theoretical consequences of such a conversion that exception is to be taken. In making the conversion abstraction is made from whatever elements do not lend themselves to its terms; which amounts to abstracting from precisely those elements of business that have an institutional force and that therefore would lend themselves to scientific inquiry of the modern kind -- those (institutional) elements whose analysis might contribute to an understanding of modern business and of the life of the modern business community as contrasted with the assumed primordial hedonistic calculus.

25

The point may perhaps be made clearer. Money and the habitual resort to its use are conceived to be simply the ways and means by which consumable goods are acquired, and therefore simply a convenient method by which to procure the pleasurable sensations of consumption; these latter being in hedonistic theory the sole and overt end of all economic endeavor. Money values have therefore no other significance than that of purchasing power over consumable goods, and money is simply an expedient of computation. Investment, credit extensions, loans of all kinds and degrees, with payment of interest and the rest, are likewise taken simply as intermediate steps between the pleasurable sensations of consumption and the efforts induced by the anticipation of these sensations, other bearings of the case being disregarded. The balance being kept in terms of the hedonistic consumption, no disturbance arises in this pecuniary traffic so long as the extreme terms of this extended hedonistic equation -- pain-cost and pleasure-gain -- are not altered, what lies between these extreme terms being merely algebraic notation employed for convenience of accountancy. But such is not the run of the facts in modern business. Variation of capitalization, e.g., occur without its being practicable to refer them to visibly equivalent variations either in the state of the industrial arts or in the sensations of consumption. Credit extensions tend to inflation of credit, rising prices, overstocking of markets, etc., likewise without a visible or securely traceable correlation in the state of the industrial arts or in the pleasures of consumption; that is to say, without a visible basis in those material elements to which the hedonistic theory reduces all economic phenomena. Hence the run of the facts, in so far, must be thrown out of the theoretical formulation. The hedonistically presumed final purchase of consumable goods is habitually not contemplated in the pursuit of business enterprise. Business men habitually aspire to accumulate wealth in excess of the limits of practicable consumption, and the wealth so accumulated is not intended to be converted by a final transaction of purchase into consumable goods or sensations of consumption. Such commonplace facts as these, together with the endless web of business detail of a like pecuniary character, do not in hedonistic theory raise a question as to how these conventional aims, ideals, aspirations, and standards have come into force or how they affect the scheme of life in business or outside of it; they do not raise the questions because such questions cannot be answered in the terms which the hedonistic economists are content to use, or, indeed, which their premises permit them to use. The question which arises is how to explain the facts away; how theoretically to neutralize them so that they will not have to appear in the theory, which can then be drawn indirect and unambiguous terms of rational hedonistic calculation. They are explained away as being aberrations due to oversight or lapse of memory on the part of business men, or to some failure of logic or insight. Or they are construed and interpreted into the rationalistic terms of the hedonistic calculus by resort to an ambiguous use of the hedonistic concepts. So that the whole "money economy", with all the machinery of credit and the rest, disappears in a tissue of metaphors to reappear theoretically expurgated, sterilized, and simplified into a "refined system of barter", culminating in a net aggregate maximum of pleasurable sensations of consumption.

But since it is in just this unhedonistic, unrationalistic pecuniary traffic that the tissue of business life consists, since it is this peculiar conventionalism of aims and standards that differentiates the life of the modern business community from any conceivable earlier or cruder phase of economic life; since it is in this tissue of pecuniary intercourse and pecuniary concepts, ideals, expedients, and aspirations that the conjunctures of business life arise and run their course of felicity and devastation; since it is here that those institutional changes take place which distinguish one phase or era of the business community's life from any other; since the growth and change of these habitual, conventional elements make the growth and character of any business era or business community; any theory of business which sets these elements aside or explains them away misses the main facts which it has gone out to seek. Life and its conjunctures and institutions being of this complexion, however much that state of the case may be depreciated, a theoretical account of the phenomena of this life must be drawn in these terms in which the phenomena occur. It is not simply that the hedonistic interpretation of modern economic phenomena is inadequate or misleading; if the phenomena are subjected to the hedonistic interpretation in the theoretical analysis they disappear from the theory; and if they would bear the interpretation in fact they would disappear in fact. If, in fact, all the conventional relations and principles of pecuniary intercourse were subject to such a perpetual rationalized, calculating revision, so that each article of usage, appreciation, or procedure must approve itself de novo on hedonistic grounds of sensuous expediency to all concerned at every move, it is not conceivable that the institutional fabric would last over night.

www.ingramcontent.com/pod-product-compliance
Lightning Source LLC
Chambersburg PA
CBHW022057190326
41520CB00008B/800